Rain

Rain

Poems

Leslie E. Porter

Leaf Catching Press

Cover Art by Leslie E. Porter
Illustrations and photographs by Leslie E. Porter

Published in the United States of America
by Leaf Catching Press
leafcatchingpress@gmail.com

ISBN: 979-8-218-36522-6

For the clouds in my tea,
for yesterday's tears that have become rain,
thank you
Thich Nhat Hanh, for teaching me about these wonders

HOME

where is home?
does home float in the heavy humid hometown air of 1991
perfumed with the diaphanous blue of late spring?
is it cosmic - a planet, a solar system, a spiral galaxy?
is it invisibly diminutive? an atom? an electron? a quark?
dark matter?
does home live in a tender hand?
a mother's hand? a mother's hand is home:
a door to the heart, always left welcomingly ajar,
a glow coating a front lawn from a porch light, left on.
is home a 16 year-old self? a house? what number would it be?
is it a hermit crab's shell, temporary, outgrown, exchanged or
is it a month? does it exist in April, a greening world?
a glass of ice water, sweating, shared on the screened porch
a handful of peanuts, crunched in the mouth, is it that taste?
is it a backyard, a lawn chair, with sun shining
on its woven plastic fabric straps?
is home a song, a smell, hot laundry pulled from a clothes dryer?
does it live on his lips, in his voice, played back
till the tape wore out?

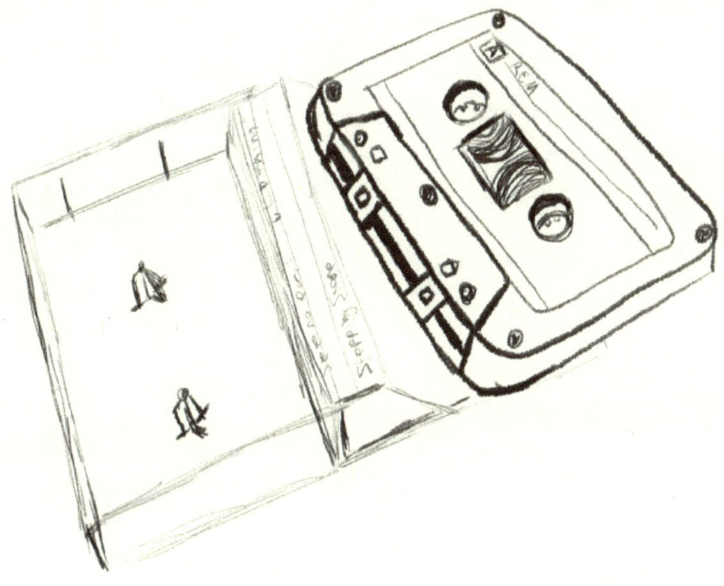
A
REM

MEMORY

You know how sometimes
When you concentrate
On a memory
That seems crystallized,
It evaporates
At the mind's touch?

Scurries away like
A rabbit after freezing
And then bolts
Like touching it
Makes it somehow recoil
Disappear

Going to that tender place
A hand in the pond
Creating ripples outward
The memory breaks
Free
Like sand dunes
Eroding
Into the
Encroaching rising
Sea

ALL THE COLORS

Did you
eat warm scones with
butter and jelly, pigeons bobbing
near the "stay off the grass"
signs?
were you there too,
somehow?

Did you walk with me in
my veins on those
same worn paths
or
did I walk with you?
were we together in light?
do you walk with me now?

GRANDMA'S CONDO IN CALIFORNIA

Had a Japanese fountain
that made an impression on me
like the swim cap
and the ukulele,
it became California

Warm air and that fountain
with its bamboo spout
waiting to be tipped by gravity
in a small green space
near the carport

An exotic element
and one of the only things I remember,
being outside
looking at that fountain
wondering how it worked

I don't know
if it had water in it
or whether it was
waiting
for rain

Rain

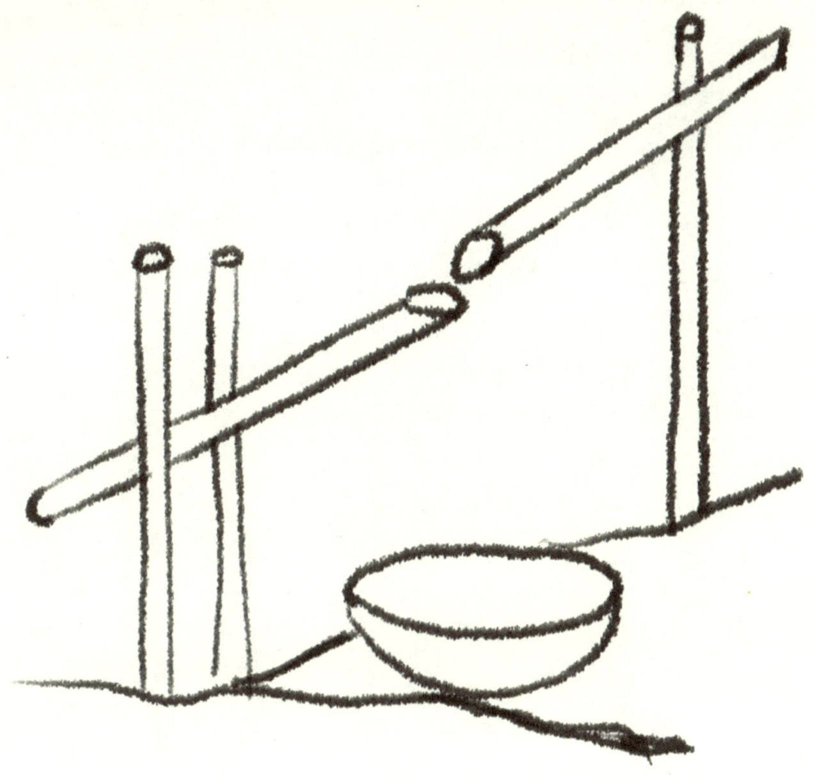

ONE DAY IN APRIL

Did you come to me or did I come to you
Or did a rainstorm bring us together
Turned around in a cornfield
(dark skies and torrents)
You touched my shoulder
(humidity steaming off water stained pavement)

I noticed your wispy brown curls waving gently in a spring breeze
And how your irises hang and hover, leaving a white cushion
above your waterline
Your steady gaze, seeing me
We said our hellos and goodbyes
And you drove off
Leaving me watching from the sidewalk
To remember the rain

Rain

PORTRAIT OF HARDWOOD ISLAND, MAINE, SUMMER 1992

Like a sun worn polaroid snapshot crumpled and blurred,
Cells replaced
A self no longer alive imprinted
On a tiny island off the coast

Black flies threatened
Cold mornings opened with pancakes
Old wood that smelled of flannel and other girls, other summers,
trunks full of their memories, their hot tea, their incandescent
phosphorescent fish in the moonlight

Wait

In quiet dark woods walking alone I get tripped by a root.
I fall, laid out in moss.
I feel the forest talking, breathing, my face at ground level.
It is a presence.
I take off my headphones and walk,
frightened into unblocking one barrier.

The island is so full it scares me, grabs me, shakes me.

I reach the other side and see rock cliffs and sunshine.
I look for butterflies to capture and release.
I wear long sleeves and long pants.
I never get bitten by a black fly.

I go to bonfires on a rocky beach, stones smooth, heavy, gray.
I see the Northern Lights but I don't remember them, wondering now

how I could forget

My past self saw them and wrote about them in a letter to my mom.
She kept it and read it to me.
I've never seen anything like it, I said.

Those memories are unreachable, encoded somewhere else,
inaccessible. The letter, gone.

But I remember the cold beach.
The sky full of stars.
The bunk near the window.
Being shaken awake.

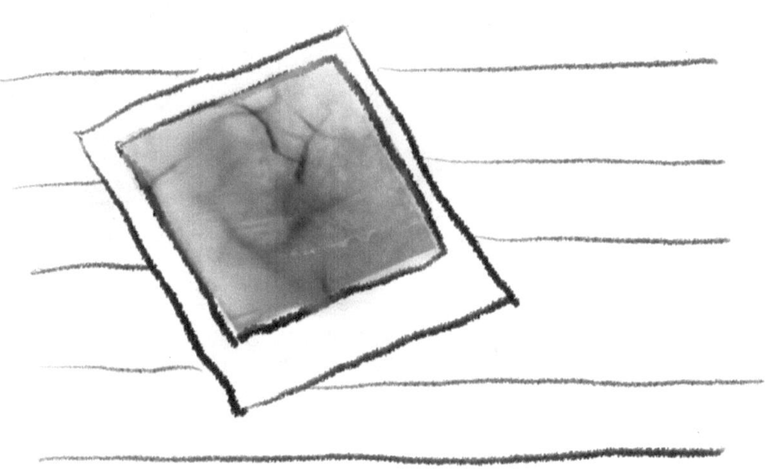

ONCOMING STORM

fever of a hot night
broken
by a chance meeting
of fronts,
their electrons pinballing.
my curtains
billow,
signaling relief.

thunderstorm winds
wash over me

the wooden bar
weighting my fabric blinds
flails wildly in this rush,
meeting window sill wood,
persistently knocking
calling, rapping,
asking, asking, asking,
the same question.

Rain

SUMMER IN THE BACKYARD

drooping dotted beauties, little snowy dewdrops: lily of the valley,
appear big bang like, as if out of nowhere and nothing,
and yet they appear
encircling a hamlet and making it holy,
a place not to be stepped on, too dense for feet

this humble backyard
steeped in starry pinkish perfection: mountain laurel
with a drainpipe sunk in its center
held huge yellow banana slugs
arising after a rain, ripe to discover.

LEAF CATCHING

On glittering Saturdays
when the sky was a piercing, cold blue
full of marching clouds that didn't hold rain,
we would go leaf catching

waiting for a great wind to start a deluge
sending leaves spinning down, swirling,
twisting and curling, we would fling our bodies
delighting in the squall

peeling our jackets and sweatshirts off,
electrified by our own energy,
until we were down to our t-shirts,
sweaty and proud in autumn's darkening cold

Rain

NEIGHBORHOOD

We are constellations on
Each other's maps
Walls become membranes
Wood and cement soften
Into tissue
Water trickles, earthy tears drip into storm drains
Taking leaves down to gather at the bottom of our street

We are like birds murmuring
Behaving like cells part of a larger biological whole
Manifestations manifesting

The road, sidewalks, pathways
Are veins through which
We all travel
And exchange something - what?
Hear each other's hearts beat and break

(Hold on)

See the glow of each other's porch lights
Streaming out
Little warm canyons
For our grief to channel
For our hearts to ford
Reflecting Light on one another
Through this strange journey

Rain

IF I WANT TO

Be free as a spider who spins her web carefully, carrying knowing:
inherited inherent wisdom of generations living within,
let the salt of my skin be sipped by the last flies of fall
as wind quivers with a few lonely wasps of November, as
sun sinks into my open arms
if I want to

To adorn myself with words formed out of dandelion crowns
to write dark letters on each rising marble stair
to be in the day all day
distill dewdrops from morning wind
translate them into music note by note
if I want to

To weave sunlight, squirrels' tails and bike wheels
pavement and grass: hew them
grind my knees with them
feel dirt in my teeth
shape and spell a dervish's dance dripping on braiding fingers
if I want to

Sit and say nothing or
utter Truth's name or
leave everything nameless,
turn colors into forms,
speak them out loud: yes.
if I want to.

Rain

STARS SET

invisible at predawn
as we gather at the sliding door and edge ourselves up
to the cold glass behind swaying vertical blinds
the moon's crescent body hides its dark whole,
a secret husk rattling and dry
visible against a still black sky
as day's thin line rises clear and cerulean
leaves fall insistently, flecking
yellow drops
on frosty ground

MARS IN MOONGLOW

In the light just below
Sunrise
Blue brightness edged with
Red
The crust of Earth
Seems to be rising up
A belly breathing in beneath the horizon
Glowing from inside out
Temporal burn
And there is Mars
Bright, distinct
Winking, persistent
Alive in Light

Rain

COLORS, SKY

sweeping blues a backdrop for
aching muted yellows
awash in sleeting clouds
beating back slushy grays
simmering above that teasing smell of mud in winter
late afternoon sun hitting angled rooftops
divided by the sliding sound of supermarket doors
serving as a threshold between
worlds

THERE WAS THUNDER

There was a mosquito buzzing
There was rain
And darkness
And still stillness
And stuffiness and
Heat. And
Now there is morning
And fog burning off
And a hint of cool
On a humid breeze
And leaves scraping across the sidewalk
And sky and green umbrellas
And a tinge of red
At the ends of maple branches

Rain

WIND IN TREES

is a balm
a tincture
an endlessly refilling cup of
simultaneous sunlit moonlight
(oxygen bubbling up from sea algae)
towering oaks reach up
dropping acorns

wind in trees
on skin is
a motion salve
a golden ferry traveling
between ports

Rain

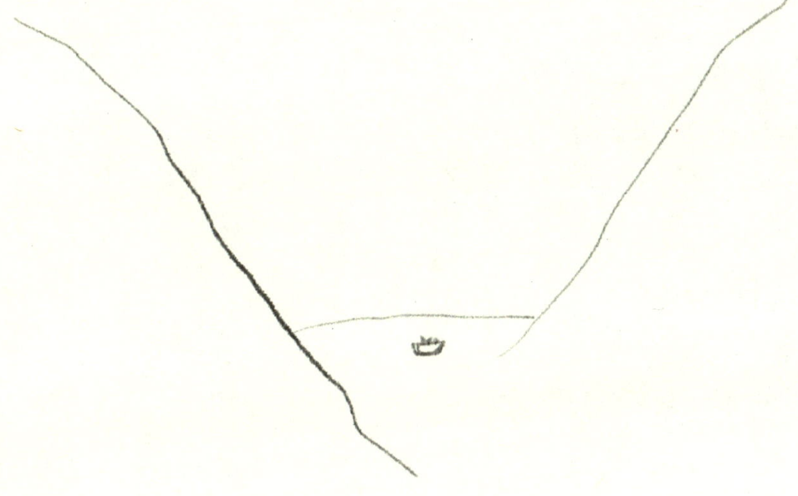

FLOCK

Specks in the sky flecks
In flight
In my photo
Just blurs
Not representative of
Their transcendent
Movement - the dance -
Of a flock of black
Across a near night
Sky
A sky that can't decide
Between brightening
And rain

These black birds
Paint
Today's final daylight
Glories
In their own
Image

CRICKET CHIRPS

Cricket chirps remind that it
is still August even as this
pen drags across
this page
as fingers strike typewriter keys
pounding out repetitions
alone in the kitchen
clacking away
with screen door slamming
cicadas humming
wings rattling
unspecific insects invisibly
chanting mantras
time passing totems
stacked on an uneasy history
of rock and soil
and shifting crusts

LATE SUMMER NIGHT

Same soft light same warmth
humidity hangs out deep, stretched,
a quilt on a clothesline, drenched by an
afternoon cloudburst
doesn't have the delicate ease of a spring
night
has a hangdog look
has a tired feel
like an exiting,
a departure,
waving from
the terminal

Rain

A RAIN FOSSIL AT DINOSAUR STATE PARK

To run a hand over million year old mud is to be reminded
of commonality.

To find one moment of splooshing and splashing
and pock marked earth cradling those drops
in a heavy embrace is to feel
a kinship.

Echoing impacts resemble tree bark or reptile skin
but they are something else - a texture of Earth skin,
darkened and smoothed fragments of another creature's daylight, or
dreams.

Impressions of clouds that floated over distant disparate heads prompt
questions:
What did they think, then, in a pelting rain? Was it a hot rain? Or cold?
Did they shiver? Did they seek shelter?

To touch the fingerprints of a moment is to be
a visitor,
and we are all visitors.

ALL OF US

Life's need for life
A driving drum
A meteor shower
A cellular memory handed down from algal ancestors
A get up
A call to action
First rays last rays all
Light
Everything everything
Green possibility
A blazing hot core in all of us
All beings
Radiating outward

ABOUT THE AUTHOR

Leslie E. Porter is a poet, artist, outdoor educator, nature journaling instructor, librarian, beginning guitarist, and continual student of the world.

Instagram: @cloudsinhertea
Email: leafcatchingpress@gmail.com

www.ingramcontent.com/pod-product-compliance
Lightning Source LLC
LaVergne TN
LVHW091239150826
845673LV00003B/1224

* 9 7 9 8 2 1 8 3 6 5 2 2 6 *